IS CHICKEN SOUP JEWISH?
Questions and Answers for Jewish Kids

by
Rabbi Rafael Grossman

Mazo Publishers

Is Chicken Soup Jewish?
Questions and Answers for Jewish Kids

ISBN 978-1-956381-344
LCCN: 2023932014

by Rabbi Rafael Grossman
Developed by Anna Olswanger

Copyright © Estate of Shirley Zaretsky Grossman, 2023
Illustration copyright © Joshua M. Edelglass, 2023
Colorization copyright © Sivan Buntova, 2023

Mazo Publishers
www.mazopublishers.com
Email: info@mazopublishers.com

Design and Layout by ER Studios

Image Credits

Cover illustration and interior adapted versions
  by Joshua M. Edelglass

Colorized images of Rabbi Rafael Grossman
  by Sivan Buntova

Photograph of the Baron Hirsch synagogue used
  with permission of Baron Hirsch Congregation: 24

Images from Mazo Publishers: 19, 21, 27, 29, 33

Images from Israel Gov't Press Office: 34, 38

Images from Wiki Commons: 12, 15, 16, 17, 19, 26, 47, 49

5432
All rights reserved.
No part of this publication may be translated, reproduced, stored in a retrieval system, or transmitted in any form or by any means, electronic, mechanical, photocopying, recording or otherwise, without prior permission in writing from the publisher.

To ask a question is a positive admission that you do not know something, and are willing to look to someone else to help you discover the answer.

Lesson learned from the Passover Haggadah

Contents

Introduction – 7
A Note to Parents and Teachers – 9

Chapter One – 11
The Jewish Holidays
*Passover • Rosh Hashanah • Yom Kippur
Sukkot • Chanukah • Purim*

Chapter Two – 23
The Synagogue

Chapter Three – 28
Israel

Chapter Four – 35
Jews in America

Chapter Five – 41
Jewish Family Life
Birth / Early Life • Adolescence • Adulthood • Death

Chapter Six – 52
Jewish Beliefs
Religion • Science • The Bible • Food

Chapter Seven – 63
The Jewish People

A Final Word from Rabbi Grossman to Kids – 68
Rabbi Rafael G. Grossman – 69

Introduction

Whether you go to a day school or public school, you are bound to have friends who are not Jewish or Jewish friends who want to know more about Judaism. Sometimes they might ask you a question or two about something in Jewish life that's been on their mind. For example, they might ask why Jews go to the synagogue on Saturday or if chicken soup is something Jewish. If you show your friends a book with Hebrew writing, they might want to know why the letters look strange or even funny.

But just because you're Jewish doesn't mean you know all the answers – yet.

So, to help you get prepared, Rabbi Rafael Grossman wrote this book with answers to more than 180 questions. While some of the questions might seem basic to the Jewish way of life, these are the questions that the non-Jewish or non-religious Jewish kids might ask.

Rabbi Grossman was always answering questions about Judaism. He was a rabbi in Texas, New Jersey, and in Memphis, Tennessee, at a synagogue that was once the largest Orthodox synagogue in the country and in the middle of a city filled with non-Jews of all races.

Rabbi Grossman mixed with everyone. He spoke at prayer breakfasts with pastors. He was on the Steering Committee of the National Conference of Christians and Jews. He worked with local politicians to support Israel, Soviet Jewry, and to fight anti-Semitism, and those politicians were often Christian, Black and white, and included the Tennessee governor, Tennessee senators, U.S. congressmen, U.S. senators, and even the U.S. vice-president. He worked with the Interfaith Affairs department of the Anti-Defamation League and spoke at Christian conventions like the Southern Baptist Convention. He answered questions on city-wide call-in radio shows.

Introduction

Rabbi Rafael Grossman was invited to be the Guest Chaplain in the U.S. House of Representatives, 2001.

Rabbi Grossman didn't just answer questions from adults. He answered questions from kids, the non-Jewish ones who came to his synagogue on Sunday School tours with their church groups, and the Jewish kids who attended his *"kumsitz"* programs.

He answered questions from kids everywhere.

On the following pages, you will discover how Rabbi Grossman answered all the questions, and how his answers will help you, too.

A Note to Parents and Teachers

My father, Rabbi Rafael Grossman, was a distinguished scholar and educator, a rabbi with a vast congregation, a leader of major Jewish organizations, a champion for interdenominational understanding and an activist for human rights. Yet, if you waited in line with him at the supermarket, he instantly became your friend. There was no person my father would not engage in conversation with. No matter whether it was a child or a homeless person, he knew there was a soul inside yearning to be nurtured, a kinship waiting to be formed. He sought to enrich his own life by speaking to others.

Rabbi Grossman with Israeli soldiers

He didn't shy away from the questions that young people asked because he knew that when they became adults, they would need to think about who they are and where they came from. He believed that if you never learned the alphabet, you would never be able to read, let alone write. In this book I constantly hear my father's voice, his profound philosophy, his engaging warmth and honesty, his fierce passion to teach, all powered by his unswerving commitment to tradition.

Some questions here are truly basic such as *"Why Hebrew?"* Yet, my father takes thousands of years of scholarship and boundless volumes of intricate Jewish legal text to develop intelligible and digestible answers. Though written for young people, there is tremendous scholarship in this book. My father believed that kids can understand and be empowered by a knowledge of Judaism. He would never talk down to his audience and would always assume that his listeners had a healthy knowledge of the English language. He would often remind us that knowledge is humankind's most powerful tool and "the most joyous human experience."

In my mind this book should be mandatory reading for every Jew regardless of age, denomination or level of scholarship. My father asks us all to question and to seek answers. He asks us to educate ourselves so we can educate others, to better ourselves so we can better the world. When my father was asked, "What's the purpose in being Jewish," he answered, "It's the repair of the world. *Tikkun olam.*" He thought we should make this world the best place we can – if possible, forever. For him, Judaism was life, and it enabled him to value every moment and every person.

Rabbi Dr. Shamai Grossman
Ra'anana, Israel

CHAPTER ONE

THE JEWISH HOLIDAYS

Passover

WHAT ARE THOSE BIG CRACKERS JEWS EAT ON PASSOVER?

They're called "*matzot.*" They're not really crackers, but thin loaves of unleavened bread.

WHY DO YOU EAT THEM?

All Jewish holidays, including Passover, are reenactments of biblical stories. The book of Exodus describes how the Israelites were slaves in Egypt for over two hundred years and how they suffered under the Egyptian kings, called pharaohs. (For example, one pharaoh ordered all Israelite baby boys to be drowned.) Then God chose Moses to lead

Chapter One

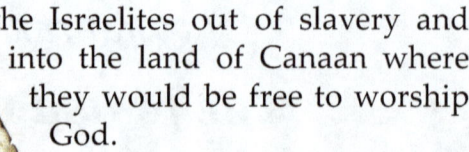
Matzah

the Israelites out of slavery and into the land of Canaan where they would be free to worship God.

After a number of miracles, including the ten plagues described in several chapters of Exodus, the pharaoh ordered the Israelites to leave Egypt. But they were afraid he would change his mind, and left in the middle of the night with their unbaked bread on their heads. The hot desert sun baked it into thin loaves, similar to the matzah we eat today. Eating matzah on Passover reminds us of the suffering of our ancestors in Egypt, and their journey into freedom.

What does the word "matzah" mean?

Unleavened Bread. It's the singular of *"matzot."*

Are they Hebrew words?

Yes. In fact, another word you might hear is *"Pesach,"* which is the Hebrew word for Passover.

Why do you use Hebrew words when you talk about Judaism?

Because the language of the Torah is Hebrew. Using Hebrew words keeps the Torah part of our daily lives.

So can you eat matzah any time or just at Passover?

You can eat matzah every day if you want. Some kids like taking peanut butter and matzah sandwiches to school for lunch.

Rosh Hashanah and Yom Kippur

Why do you celebrate the Jewish New Year in September instead of January?

The actual beginning of the Jewish year is in the spring on the first day of the month of Nisan, right before Passover. That marks the time when the Jews were about to leave Egypt, about 3300 years ago, and enter their new life as a free people. The New Year you're asking about, when Jews review their personal deeds, occurs at the end of the summer on the first two days of the seventh month, Tishrei. It's called Rosh Hashanah. We believe God created the first human on Rosh Hashanah, so we take account of ourselves then. It's also the Day of Judgment, and ten days later, on Yom Kippur, we ask God to judge us favorably and to forgive us.

You keep saying the names of months in Hebrew. Where do the names come from?

The Jewish year is divided into months according to the number of times the moon revolves around the earth, which happens to be twelve. (An extra month is inserted in a leap year.) The Hebrew names of these months come from the Talmud.

What does "Rosh Hashanah" mean?

Literally translated, it means "the head of the year."

What does "Yom Kippur" mean?

It means "Day of Atonement." It's the day we ask for atonement, or forgiveness.

How do you know if you're forgiven on Yom Kippur?

You have to hope in your heart that you are. But

basically, we believe that God forgives all sins committed against Him, though not sins committed against other people. Before Yom Kippur, many Jews ask those they may have offended to forgive them.

Why do Jews fast on Yom Kippur?

So we can concentrate on praying and on receiving forgiveness.

Do you pray in the synagogue or at home?

We spend Yom Kippur in the synagogue. That keeps us focused on the day's holiness, and on our connection with other Jews.

Who says you have to fast on Yom Kippur?

We believe God ordered us to fast. In the book of Leviticus is the verse, "On the tenth day of the seventh month you shall afflict your souls." The rabbis in the Talmud interpreted this to mean fasting and avoiding other pleasures, like bathing.

You mean you can't take a bath on Yom Kippur?

Afraid not.

Do you fast on other days or just Yom Kippur?

We fast on five other days, but for different reasons. For example, on the ninth day of the Hebrew month of Av, both the first and second Temples in Jerusalem were destroyed and the Jewish people were taken prisoners, first by the Babylonians and then by the Romans. So that's a day of national mourning, and a day of praying that such tragedies won't happen again. Like on Yom Kippur, we fast to help us pray. The other fast days are the 10th of Tevet, the 17th of Tammuz, the 3rd of Tishrei, and the Fast of Esther on the 13th day of Adar, the day before Purim.

WHY DO YOU FAST ON THE OTHER FOUR DAYS YOU MENTIONED?

On the 10th of Tevet the Babylonians laid siege to Jerusalem, and on the 17th of Tammuz they broke through Jerusalem's walls.

A remnant of the First Temple period wall in Jerusalem can still be seen today, probably similar to the section the Babylonians laid siege to on the 10th of Tevet.

On the 3rd of Tishrei, Gedalia, the Babylonian-appointed Jewish governor of Jerusalem was assassinated.

All three fast days in general mark the expulsion of the Jews from Judea, and their persecution and suffering.

On the 13th day of Adar, the Jews of Persia fasted and prayed to defeat Haman, a wicked man who plotted to murder the Jews.

DO KIDS ALSO FAST?

Yes. A Jewish boy accepts his religious duties at the age of thirteen, and in order to prepare himself, starts fasting at the age of twelve. A girl accepts her religious duties at the age of twelve, so she starts fasting at the age of eleven.

Chapter One

Sukkot

WHAT IS THAT HUT I SOMETIMES SEE IN THE YARDS OF JEWISH HOMES?

It's called a sukkah.

DO YOU CAMP OUT THERE?

In a sense, yes. During the week-long festival of Sukkot, which comes a few days after Yom Kippur, we eat our meals in the sukkah and invite guests over. Some people

While a sukkah can be built in many different sizes and styles, with all kinds of decorations, there are guidelines for a sukkah according to Jewish law, such as making sure the materials used for the roof have been grown, like tree branches or bamboo stalks.

sleep in the sukkah at night. We spend as much time as we can in the sukkah because it reminds us that when we journeyed in the desert after being freed from slavery and only had temporary huts to live in, God watched over us and protected us.

BUT JUST BECAUSE JEWS LIVED IN A SUKKAH A LONG TIME AGO, WHY DO YOU NEED TO DO IT TODAY?

Like Passover, Sukkot is a holiday that is a reenactment of a biblical story, in this case, the forty years that the Jews spent living in huts in the desert with only God's protection. Jews never wrote history books, but instead, through the Torah's commandments, we live history. That way, we really remember it and feel it ourselves.

During Sukkot, there are four plants, called arba'at ha-minim, that are relevant to the holiday and a part of the synagogue service. There is the citron (etrog) [A] and the frond of a date palm (lulav) [B] joined with the willow (aravah) [C] and myrtle (hadass) [D].

Chanukah

IS CHANUKAH THE SAME AS CHRISTMAS, BUT FOR JEWS?

Chanukah has nothing to do with Christmas. Chanukah is a minor national and religious holiday that marks the victory 2000 years ago of a small group of Jews, called Maccabees, over their Syrian oppressors. The Syrians, who occupied the land of Israel at the time, tried to force the Jews to worship idols. Through guerrilla warfare, the Jews defeated their enemies.

IS IT OKAY IF I SEND CHRISTMAS CARDS TO MY JEWISH FRIENDS?

It's really pointless, the same as if a Jew were to send a Chanukah card to a Christian friend. By the way, Christians don't offend Jews by *not* sending them Christmas cards.

WHY DO YOU HAVE SO MANY DAYS IN CHANUKAH?

Chanukah is more than the celebration of a military victory. When the Maccabees won their guerrilla war against the Syrians, they wanted to restore Jewish worship to the Temple. The enemy had brought in idols and other forbidden things, like pigs. The Maccabees decided to rekindle the menorah and show that the flame of Judaism burned again. They needed a pure oil that had never been used for idolatrous purposes or been mixed with other oils. They found a cruse of olive oil with the high priest's seal on it from the days before the Syrian occupation (the seal guaranteed the oil's purity), but there was only enough to last one day. A miracle happened. The oil lasted eight days, so on Chanukah, we light one candle the first night and an additional candle each night until we light eight candles.

WHAT'S A "CRUSE?"

A little jar.

On the last night of Chanukah, eight candles are lit for the holiday. The extra, raised candle, called the Shamash, is a helper candle for the other candles. The candle holder can be designed in many different creative styles and is called a Menorah or Chanukiah.

WHAT DO YOU DO WHILE THE CHANUKAH CANDLES ARE BURNING?

Well, one thing we do is play dreidel.

Chapter One

WHAT'S DREIDEL?

The Dreidel

The Syrians outlawed the teaching of Judaism, so Jewish children had to go into the woods to learn Torah. When the Syrian soldiers came near, the children pretended they were playing a game that used a spinning top, what was later called a *"dreidel"* in Yiddish. To commemorate the courage of these children and their teachers, we play with a similar spinning top during Chanukah today. Our dreidel has four Hebrew letters, one on each side, which represent the Hebrew words, "A great miracle happened there." Interestingly, when children play this game in Israel, their dreidel has one Hebrew letter that is different, to represent the Hebrew words, "A great miracle happened *here*."

WHY DON'T JEWS CELEBRATE CHRISTMAS?

Why don't Christians celebrate Chanukah? Bear in mind that Judaism began almost 2,000 years before Christianity, and we Jews simply practice our religion as we've always known it.

WHY DON'T JEWS BELIEVE IN JESUS?

The Jewish Messiah as described in the books of Isaiah, Jeremiah, and Malachi will be a human being who ushers in world peace. Since we are still waiting for world peace, and since, according to the Torah, God would never appear as a human being, Jews can't accept Jesus as the Messiah.

WHY WOULDN'T GOD APPEAR AS A HUMAN BEING?

Because of the verse Exodus 33:20 which says, "You cannot see My face, for no human can see Me and live."

Purim

SOMETIMES I SEE MY JEWISH FRIENDS DRESS UP IN COSTUMES. IS THIS ANOTHER JEWISH HOLIDAY?

Yes. After the destruction of the First Temple, the Jews of Persia were ruled by King Ahasuerus and his viceroy Haman. Haman wanted to murder the Jews of Persia.

But the Jewish Queen Esther, with the help of her Uncle Mordecai, persuaded Ahasuerus to intercede. For legal reasons, Ahasuerus couldn't cancel the murderous decree he had been tricked into signing, but he could issue a new one. It allowed the Jews to defend themselves against Haman's army. Not one Jew died in the battle. That day became the holiday of Purim. The word *"Purim"* means lots (like a raffle) because Haman threw lots to determine the month the Jews would be killed. It was the month of Adar, a few weeks before Passover.

But why do you dress up in costumes?

The Talmud says that on Purim you should turn things around. You should be so happy that you can't tell the difference between "Cursed is Haman!" and "Blessed is Mordecai!" Kids especially like to dress up in costumes that day so that no one can tell who they are.

What's the most important Jewish holiday?

Interestingly enough, the Talmud says that the only holiday to exist after the Messiah comes will be Purim. This seems strange because the book in the Bible that describes Purim is the Scroll of Esther, and it's the only book in the Bible that doesn't mention God's name. But Purim was the time when Jews set aside their personal differences, fasted, prayed for God's help, and took up swords against Haman's army. So the Talmud considers Purim the most important Jewish holiday. But Purim is not the holiest day. The holiest day for Jews is the Sabbath.

Chapter Two

The Synagogue

I've seen lots of synagogues from the outside, but what do they look like on the inside? Like churches?

No. Synagogues are miniature replications of the ancient Temple, which stood in Jerusalem. That's why synagogues face the direction of Jerusalem. (In America, that means the east.) Today's Orthodox synagogues, for example, have separate sections for men and women, like in the Temple. They have an Ark, the container for the Torah scroll, and an Eternal Light, or *"ner tamid,"* which symbolizes the Torah, the light we live by. Although in ancient times this was an oil-burning lamp (the Temple priests continually replenished the olive oil), today the *ner tamid* is an electric light bulb.

Synagogues also have a candelabra, or *"menorah,"* another symbol of the Torah's light, and a high place, or

Inside the Baron Hirsch Synagogue, where Rabbi Rafael Grossman served for almost 30 years as Rabbi of the congregation.

"*bimah,*" where the Torah is read aloud four times during the week – on Monday, Thursday, Saturday mornings, and Saturday afternoons.

What's an "Orthodox" synagogue anyway?

A synagogue that accepts the laws of the Bible as interpreted by the Talmud, the "oral law."

Is that the kind of synagogue you belong to?

Yes. There are also Conservative and Reform synagogues.

Why?

Two reasons. I would like to practice Judaism exactly as Jews have practiced it throughout the ages. And I find myself fulfilled in a deep way by what Orthodox Judaism teaches.

What exactly does it teach you?

That things change in this world, but not God's laws.

Do all Jews, or just Orthodox Jews, go to synagogue on Saturday instead of Sunday?

All Jews.

Why?

Because Jewish observance is based on laws in the Torah, the first part of what Christians call the Old Testament. In Genesis, the first book of the Torah, we read how God created the universe in six days, and then rested on the seventh. The seventh day is Saturday, the Sabbath ("*Shabbat*" in Hebrew), and since God rested on Shabbat, we do too. That means we avoid what the Torah calls "labors" (writing letters and handling money, for example). And in honor of Shabbat, we attend synagogue services.

What do you do there?

We listen to a reader chant the weekly Torah portion, just as it was chanted in the ancient Temple of Solomon. The first portion, Genesis 1:1-6:8, is chanted right after Rosh Hashanah. The readings continue for an entire year until all five books of Moses have been completed.

We pray, of course. And in many synagogues we listen to a rabbi explain the weekly Torah portion and how it applies to what is happening in the world. Then we socialize. We meet our friends after services and enjoy each other's company.

Can you say your own prayers in the synagogue?

You can, but that's in addition to the regular service.

When you pray, where do the prayers come from?

We read them from a book called the "*siddur.*" Some of

The Torah

the prayers are Psalms, which we believe were written by King David. Others were compiled by Rabbis 1500 to 2000 years ago.

You said that the Torah portion is chanted just as it was during the time of Solomon. How do you know how it was chanted?

In synagogue Bibles, under and above the various Hebrew letters and words, are musical notes called "cantillation." The sounds of these notes have been handed down from father to son for generations, although Jews in different parts of the world sing the notes a little differently.

Can a kid who's not Jewish visit a synagogue?

Anyone can visit. In fact, the prophet Isaiah wrote, "For my house shall be a house of prayer unto all people."

Is there a rule that Jews have to go to synagogue on the Sabbath?

Being a Jew is being part of the Jewish people, so we find it more joyous to share Shabbat with others.

Also, we know from the verse in Psalms, "Many people are the glory of God," that we pay tribute to God if we go to the synagogue. But if you're sick or not able to go for another reason, you could say most, though not all, of the service at home.

My church has pictures of Jesus on the walls. What do you put on your walls? Pictures of Old Testament heroes?

A synagogue doesn't have pictures of humans, just as the Temple didn't have carvings or paintings of humans. That's to show that Jews worship only God.

This picture shows the Torah Ark in the Renanim Synagogue in Jerusalem. This synagogue was relocated from Padua, Italy together with its 18th-century Ark, ner tamid, and bimah to the Heichal Shlomo building in 1958.

Chapter Three

ISRAEL

Is Israel the same country today that it was in the Bible?

It's located in the same place, yes.

What language do the people in Israel speak?

The Jews there speak Hebrew. It's a very old language, of course. A man by the name of Ben Yehudah modernized it. In ancient Hebrew there were no words for things we know today, like electricity, but he didn't have to create completely new words because he took words from the Bible that represented something similar. For example, the biblical word for lightning became the modern Hebrew word for electricity.

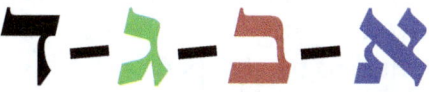

The first four letters of the Hebrew Alphabet: Aleph-Bet-Gimmel-Dalet. Hebrew is read from Right to Left.

WHY DOES HEBREW LOOK SO FUNNY?

The characters may look different, but linguists tell us that the Hebrew alphabet is the ancestor of our modern English alphabet. Hebrew is different in a way you may not be aware of, though. In English and the European languages, we read from left to right, but in Hebrew we read from right to left.

WERE THE ISRAELITES AND THE JEWS THE SAME PEOPLE?

Yes. The Jews were called Hebrews in the days of Abraham, Isaac and Jacob. The translation of the word "Hebrews" is "wanderers" because the people wandered from place to place. Later, the Jews were called Israelites because after Jacob wrestled with an angel, he was given the name "Israel," which means "Prince of God." And much later, after King David established the kingdom of Judea, the people were called Judeans, in short, Jews.

WHEN THE JEWS WENT TO THE PROMISED LAND, WHAT WERE THEY CALLED?

Israelites, because they were the children of "Israel."

WHY DID THEY KILL SO MANY OF THE PEOPLE WHO LIVED THERE?

God told them to go war against the people who lived there, called Canaanites, because they practiced idolatry and sacrificed their own children, many of them babies, to their god Moloch. The Canaanites tossed the children still alive, into fires. Just like the Nazis who murdered a million and a half children during the Holocaust had to be stopped, the Canaanites had to be stopped.

But why was the God in the Old Testament angry all the time?

God was angry at the Canaanites because they lied, stole, hoarded food, and committed murder. When the Israelites began to imitate the Canaanites and practice their religion, which included child sacrifice, God became angry at the Israelites too.

You said King David established the kingdom of Judea. Was he a Jew?

King David was a Jew because he was from the tribe of Judah and the province of Judea, but he was the king of all Israel, and the people at that time were referred to as Israelites. The kingdom was later split in two, and it wasn't until the Assyrians conquered the northern part, Israel, and only the kingdom of Judea remained, that the people became known as Jews.

Who were "the ten lost tribes?"

King David ruled over twelve tribes descended from ten of Jacob's sons and two of Jacob's grandsons. Each tribe formed a province, or state. King Solomon, David's son, also ruled over twelve tribes, as did his son Rehoboam, but then the ten tribes in the north broke away from the House of David and established their own kingdom, the Kingdom of Israel. All those who lived in this kingdom were defeated in war by the Assyrians. The ten tribes were forced to flee, and eventually disappeared. That's what we mean by the "ten lost tribes of Israel." The Bible tells us that they couldn't survive as a nation because they rebelled against God and worshipped idols.

Where are they now?

No one knows. Some people have spent their lives trying to find them. They think descendants of the ten lost tribes may be in Afghanistan, Libya, or Ethiopia but nobody's sure.

What do you think?

I think that among the Jews of today are descendants of the ten tribes. When they had to flee, some of them survived by seeking refuge in Judea. And some of them may have succeeded in practicing their Judaism wherever they went. We believe that when the Messiah comes, we will know where the ten lost tribes are, and everyone will be reunited.

If the Jews of Judea were the ones left after the kingdom split, why isn't Israel called Judea today?

Because the original name of the kingdom, before it split, was Israel.

Did the Jews in Judea have to flee, or just the Jews in Israel?

The Jews of Judea fled their land twice. First, about 586 B.C.E. ("Before the Common Era," our term for B.C.), the Babylonians conquered the land and forced many of the Jews living there into exile in Babylon. But the Babylonians were defeated in war by the Persian empire, and the Persians allowed the Jews to return to their land. Then came the Syrians, and the small group of Jews known as the Maccabees led a revolt against them. The Jews retained control of the land until the Romans came, but during two hundred years of harsh Roman occupation, many Jews again fled to Babylon.

There was never a time that Jews did not live in the land of Israel, however. They were sometimes a small community, as was the Arab community. In fact, most of the Arabs who live in Israel today came there after 1850 when Jews began to settle in larger numbers, and needed workers on their farms and in their small industries.

Are you saying that the Jews brought the Arabs in?

A majority of the Arabs, yes.

Why do the Jews and the Arabs in the Middle East keep fighting each other?

The Arabs claim that Israel belongs to them. The Jews claim the opposite, citing biblical history. They point out that not all Jews were forced to leave after the Roman conquests and that they have had a continued presence in the land that is now Israel. But the Arabs there grew into a majority. Then the state of Israel was established, based on a 1947 United Nations resolution that divided the land between Arabs and Jews. The larger part of the land was given to the Arabs, but the Arabs refused to accept a division of the land. The result was a series of tragic wars, beginning in 1948 with the War of Independence. In recent times, the Jews and the Arabs have been negotiating a peace settlement, and now that the Arabs have a government of their own within certain parts of Israel, the Jews are hopeful of a permanent peace.

Where did the Israeli flag come from?

It was originally a Zionist flag. The word "Zionist" refers to the movement, started about 100 years ago, to make Israel the Jewish homeland again. The Zionists needed a symbol, so they took what was called the Star of David, a six pointed star, and put it on a flag. They made the colors of the flag blue and white – blue representing heaven, and white representing the rest of the world (the earth and its inhabitants, regardless of their color). The idea was to bring heaven and earth together in the land that was the home of the Jewish people.

The Israeli Flag

But where did the Star of David come from?

In many of the places that archaeologists excavated in Israel they found etched in the walls six-pointed stars. These identified places where Jews either lived or were buried, so they became known as the Jewish star.

Because one tradition maintained that there were six pointed stars on the shields of King David's soldiers, it was also known as the Star of David.

What exactly does the Star of David mean?

The idea behind it is beautiful: four points represent north, south, east and west; the top point represents the heavens; and the bottom point represents the earth. The star brings them all together.

Why do some Jews wear a Star of David around their neck?

There's no religious reason for it, but probably they want to show how proud they are to be Jewish.

Is it like wearing a cross?

No. The cross is a religious symbol, but the Star of David isn't.

WHAT DO YOU MEAN IT'S NOT A RELIGIOUS SYMBOL?

It has no religious significance. The closest we can come to a religious Jewish symbol is the menorah, which represents learning, the essence of Judaism. The Torah commanded us to place a seven-branched menorah in the Tabernacle, the tent that was the center of Jewish worship before King Solomon built the Temple in Jerusalem. Its lights burned 24 hours a day to remind us of God's presence and our constant obligation to learn about Him. So when Israel was established in 1948, the government decided that the symbol of the state would be the menorah. There is a large one standing in front of Israel's parliament, the Knesset. And of course, all synagogues have a menorah on their pulpit. But a menorah is only a symbol. It's not an object of worship.

The emblem of Israel

YOU SOMETIMES SAY "US" WHEN YOU TALK ABOUT JEWS IN THE BIBLE. WHY?

The Torah was given to all Jews – the ones who stood at Mt. Sinai, and the ones not even born yet. Therefore, every Jew has to consider himself or herself as having received God's law. That's the bond which unites Jews in the present and the past. And that's why I sometimes say "us" when I talk about ancient Jews.

Chapter Four

Jews in America

Why do some people hate Jews?

Think about the kid in the class who is both little and different. The bully wants to show he's stronger, and picks on the little kid. The anti-Semite picks on the Jew. Why? Because the Jew is part of a minority, and because the Jewish religion, which is about 2,000 years older than Christianity and 2,500 years older than Islam, is different. Over the years Jews have suffered tremendously as a result.

You mean, people hate Jews because they're a minority?

People hate Jews because of what the Jewish religion teaches. And much of what it teaches, the Ten

Commandments, for example, was adopted by Christianity and Islam, but since there are three billion people in this world who claim to be Christian, and one billion who claim to be Moslem, it's easier to hate the smallest of the three religious groups – the Jews.

Why would people hate Jews because of what their religion teaches?

People know they're not supposed to murder or steal, but they do. And out of guilt they blame their problems on the Jews, the way Hitler did in the 1930's. He said that the only solution to Germany's socio-economic problems was to round up the Jews and kill them, even their children.

He ordered gas chambers and concentration camps to be built. He was responsible for the deaths of six million Jews during the second World War. People like Hitler need to blame someone else for their problems. In the case of anti-Semites, it's the Jews.

I know a kid whose parents say that Jews are money-grubbing and that they control the world. What's he supposed to do when his parents talk that way?

As much as we love our parents, we cannot keep them from catching colds, or more serious diseases. But when they do become sick, we can urge them to see doctors. Well, anti-Semitism is a disease. If we realize that our parents are suffering from this dangerous disease, one which has resulted in the deaths of millions of adults and children, we can urge them to see doctors who treat psychological disorders – psychiatrists or psychologists. At the very least we can identify the disease and realize it's something we don't want to catch. We can stay away from the ideas, and if possible, when we get older, we can explain to our parents that we won't hate.

Don't Jews hate anyone?

Individual Jews, who ignore their religious teachings or who aren't well, may hate, but not Jews as a people. Fifty years ago, when we discovered that six million of our people had been murdered in the Holocaust, we didn't hate. We didn't forgive the murderers either, because only their victims could forgive them, but we did something positive. We came back to Israel, our own land, and began to rebuild it after 2,000 years.

There are a lot of Jews in America. Why do so many of them live in New York City?

This is a land of immigrants. Few Americans landed at Plymouth Rock. Most, including Jews, landed at the port of New York and stayed because of what they found there – synagogues, friends from the old country, jobs. But there are Jews who live in different parts of the United States, in the south, the north, the west. The second largest Jewish community in the United States, almost as big as New York, is in California, in and around Los Angeles.

So where can I go to meet Jews?

You'd be surprised where Jews are. After all, we're Americans like everyone else. We don't walk around with badges saying, "We're Jews." If you want to meet Jews, find out where the closest synagogue is. I'm sure its members would be happy to meet you.

Why are certain names Jewish, like "Goldberg?"

They aren't really Jewish. Originally, people didn't have family names. They were only known by their father's name. So if my name was Benjamin and my father's name was Aaron, I was known as Benjamin-the-son-of-Aaron. However, when the Jews of Europe had to take family names, some took the names of the towns in which they lived, some the names of their professions, some the names of personal traits (like "Gross" for big), and some continued to use their father's names. For example, in families called Jacobson, the first person to adopt this name was the son-of-Jacob, or "Jacobson." There is really nothing Jewish about these names.

Do Jews in America want to live in Israel?

Many Jews do.

Why?

Some want to go there because they feel discriminated against and want to practice their Judaism in freedom. Others want to go there in order to live in the land of the fathers and mothers of their religion – Abraham, Isaac, Jacob, Sarah, Rebecca, Rachel, and Leah – and in the land of the great Jewish biblical prophets. They leave this country where they have lived quite happily and go on what is called "aliyah." Aliyah means to "go up" to the holy land of Israel.

This picture shows a group of people who made aliyah in 2014, being welcomed to Israel by Israeli President Reuven Rivlin at Ben Gurion Airport. People who make aliyah are called "Olim Chadashim – New Immigrants."

Do the Jews in America feel torn between being loyal to America and Israel?

No. All Americans have different origins. For instance, there are Americans whose grandparents or great-grandparents came from Ireland, Scotland, England, Germany, Russia, Poland, Italy, South America, Africa.

Many of these people feel a sense of loyalty or belonging to their historical home. They favor policies that are good for that country. And there is absolutely nothing wrong with that.

Americans also have different religions. There are Americans who are Catholics, Protestants, Baptists, Moslems, Buddhists, and each is loyal to others in its group. For Jews, loyalty to Israel is both loyalty to their historic home and loyalty to other Jews, but like other Americans, they are at the same time loyal to America, the land of liberty.

Also, Israel is the one country in the Middle East which, like America, is a democracy. The people there vote in free elections. And America's best friend in that part of the world is Israel. So, it's easy for an American Jew to support Israel because our own government does.

Do Jews in America speak Hebrew?

In many of the schools which Jewish children attend, they learn Hebrew, both spoken and written. But I would venture to guess that it's a small percentage of Jews outside of Israel who speak the language.

What's Yiddish? Isn't it a Jewish language?

The first Jews who migrated to Europe came through northern Germany where they absorbed the local language. When they moved on to other parts of Europe, Eastern Europe mainly, they took the language with them but spoke it with different accents and with new words. For instance, the Jews living in Russia added Russian words, the Jews in Poland added Polish words, and the Jews in Hungary, Hungarian words. Yiddish became a jargon, meaning a mixture of languages, but basically it was old German.

Did all Jews speak Yiddish?

Jews in parts of the world such as North Africa or the southern part of what was once the Soviet Union did not speak Yiddish. Nor did Jews who lived in Greece and Turkey. They spoke another language that they picked up from the people around them, a jargon called Ladino. Ladino is a mixture of Hebrew and Spanish.

Do American Jews speak Yiddish today?

Although Yiddish books and newspapers are printed in the United States, and in Israel, few Jews speak it. But there are Jews who feel it is important to preserve Yiddish because it flourished for hundreds of years in the rich Jewish culture of Eastern Europe. For those Jews, it's a bond between them and their grandparents and great-grandparents, although they may never have known them. It's also a way to communicate with Yiddish-speaking Jews outside America who don't understand English.

Chapter Five

Jewish Family Life

Birth / Early Life

Are Jewish babies baptized?

No. Baptism is a Christian practice.

So when are Jewish babies named?

A Jewish baby boy has what is called a *"brit"* on the eighth day of his life. That's when he receives his Hebrew name. A Jewish baby girl receives her Hebrew name at synagogue services, usually on the first Shabbat after her birth.

Chapter Five

Where do the names comes from?

Jewish babies are usually named after someone in the Bible or someone in the family who has died, a grandparent perhaps, whose memory the family wants to honor. And sometimes parents give their babies creative Hebrew names.

What's a creative Hebrew name?

These are names which have special meaning for the family. For example, "Aviva" is the Hebrew word for spring, and "Libby" is the Hebrew word for "my heart." Parents might name their daughter "Aviva Libby" or "spring in my heart" because spring symbolizes hope when flowers bloom and trees come back to life, and they might feel that way about their baby daughter, that she was the spring that came after the cold and bitter days of winter.

The Jewish kids I know have English names.

Maybe your friends use their Hebrew names only in the synagogue. Also, some English-sounding names like Jonathan, Miriam, and Rebecca are really Hebrew names.

What's a brit?

A circumcision.

What's a circumcision?

A circumcision is the surgical removal of the foreskin of a baby boy's penis.

Why on earth do you do that?

In the book of Genesis we read about the covenant between God and Abraham, and Abraham's descendants, the Jewish people. God promised to make the Jewish people as plentiful as the stars, to protect and guard them, and to give them a land of their own. Abraham on his part promised to keep God's commandments, including performing a *brit* on himself. "*Brit*" is the Hebrew word for promise, or covenant. Each time we circumcise a Jewish baby boy, we show our complete and total commitment to God. It's how we renew the covenant in a physical, and not just spiritual, way.

But why would God want you to do that?

Circumcision literally requires us to sacrifice a part of ourselves. People who make sacrifices tend to be more caring and loving. Maybe that's what God wants us to be.

Is a brit dangerous?

The *"mohel,"* the person who performs the *brit*, is rigorously trained not only in Jewish law, but in modern surgical techniques and antiseptics.

Do you have to be born a Jew or can you become one?

Unlike other religions, Jews don't believe in evangelizing – going out and selling the religion. But we do accept people who, on their own free will, want to become Jewish. People who have converted to Judaism are called *"gerim"* in Hebrew. In fact, some of the outstanding Jews in history were converts, like Ruth, the great-grandmother of King David.

How do you become a Jew?

First, you go to a rabbi who sets up a program of learning. Once you know the basic laws and teachings of Judaism, and are determined to live by them, you appear before three people qualified to accept conversions.

The male convert has a *brit*. Converts of both sexes immerse themselves in a small pool of water called a *"mikvah."* The converts go completely under water to show that they are separating themselves from what they have been. Then they are accepted into the Jewish faith and receive a Hebrew name.

Why do Converts get a Hebrew name?

Having a Hebrew name gives converts a religious and cultural identity among the Jewish people. As part of the name, they are called "the son of Abraham" or "the daughter of Abraham" because Abraham, the first Jew, was a convert.

Where do you go to find a mikvah?

It depends. In a small city, they're in synagogues or in a building next to them. In a large city, they're in separate buildings. You find them by doing a search for "mikvah."

You said that a convert has to learn the basic laws of Judaism. Why is learning important in Judaism? Why can't you just believe in one God and be Jewish?

Judaism is a religion based on knowledge, beginning with the written law or Torah, and continuing with the oral law or Talmud. (Jews believe that when God gave the law on Mt. Sinai, He gave it in two forms, the written and the oral.) Around the year 200 C.E., the oral law was written down in part and called the Mishnah. Several hundred years later, more of the oral law was written down, both as a commentary on and extension of the Mishnah, and called the Gemara, or Talmud. So Judaism has an incredibly vast literature full of explanations about what God wants. In order to be a practicing Jew, a person has to have some idea of what is required of her or him, and therefore has to learn. (Would you, for instance, want a doctor to operate on you if she hadn't learned anatomy in medical school?) Even a simple matter like believing in God requires learning. What do we mean by God? What does He want of us? A person can't say, "I believe in one God," and that's that. Belief has to have a purpose, a mission, and we Jews believe strongly in our mission.

What's your mission?

First of all, to be a Jew means to observe the *"mitzvot"* or commandments – Shabbat, the holidays, prayers, food laws, to name a few. In observing food laws, for example, we eat certain things, and not other things. We recite blessings before we eat and after we eat. Judaism is a demanding religion. It teaches us how to conduct our lives "when we go by the way, when we lie down, and when we rise up" – words from Deuteronomy. It's a commitment to live in a godly way. And according to Judaism, God has designated us to be the teachers of His law. Through our performance of the mitzvot, the world learns about giving, about faith, about moral and ethical behavior.

Adolescence

What's the next big event in a Jewish boy's life after his brit?

His Bar Mitzvah.

What exactly is a Bar Mitzvah?

The words "Bar Mitzvah" mean "son of the commandment." According to Judaism, when a boy reaches the age of 13, and a girl the age of 12, they become religiously mature. They are old enough to keep the Torah's commandments. For Jews, a Bar or Bat Mitzvah is an occasion for great celebration. The common practice is for a boy, when he reaches 13, to have an *"aliyah."* Aliyah means to "go up" to the high platform in the synagogue, the *bimah*, where the Torah scroll is read every Shabbat. The boy recites blessings before and after the Torah reading. Some boys chant the whole Torah portion and a special reading from one of the books of the Bible known as the Prophets. Other boys do more, such as lead the synagogue services and give a speech. And afterwards families throw parties which most rabbis don't like because the emphasis is on the wrong part of becoming a Bar Mitzvah. A lot of the meaning is lost, but people do it.

Is a Bat Mitzvah celebration the same, but for a girl?

Yes. Bat Mitzvah means "daughter of the commandment." When a girl reaches the age of 12, she is considered mature and obligated to perform the commandments required of a woman. Celebrating a Bat Mitzvah came into practice only in recent times – I'd say about 50 or 75 years ago. Today it's fairly universal among Jews. The celebration in Reform and Conservative congregations takes place in the synagogue at regular or special services. The celebration in Orthodox congregations takes place at a special service in the synagogue or at home. There's no established tradition. People create their own service. And again, the parties are not at all necessary but that's how parents express their joy at seeing their daughter reach the age of religious maturity.

Are you saying there's nothing in the Torah that requires a Bat Mitzvah?

There's nothing in the Torah that requires either a Bat or Bar Mitzvah. But we determine from the Torah that a boy at the age of thirteen, and a girl at the age of twelve, are religiously mature and obligated to observe the mitzvot. And for a boy there's a special requirement to put on tefillin during morning prayers, but not on Shabbat and the major holidays.

What's tefillin?

Those are two little black boxes with straps connected to them. One of the boxes is wrapped around the head at the hairline, and the other around the arm. They're called

Tefillin

"phylacteries" in English. This mitzvah is based on the verse in Deuteronomy, "These words, which command you this day, shall be for a sign upon your hand and for frontlets between your eyes."

What's inside the little boxes?

Parchments with the verse from Deuteronomy I just quoted, and an almost identical verse from Exodus. By wrapping the boxes around the arm (next to the heart), and around the head (next to the eyes and brain), Jewish boys and men bind their physical being to their spiritual being.

Why don't girls put on tefillin?

In Judaism, we think of God as the creator, as well as the ruler, of the world. Creativity is inherent in a woman. She's born with the natural ability to bear children, even if she can't or doesn't want to. She represents what's closest to God. So in a sense, a woman's body is set of tefillin. She's committed to God from birth.

You've said that everything Jews do is based on laws in the Torah. If there's nothing about a Bat or Bar Mitzvah in the Torah, why do you celebrate them?

The commandment to observe a Bar Mitzvah is found in the Talmud. It's extrapolated, meaning taken, from verses in the Torah.

Why is the age of religious maturity different for boys and girls?

Look around at your friends. Girls usually mature earlier than boys. They're almost adult-like when they're twelve, whereas boys are still a little babyish.

What are some of the commandments a girl takes on after she has her Bat Mitzvah?

She's required to say certain prayers each day, to recite the blessings before and after she eats, to light the Chanukah candles, to hear the reading of the Scroll of Esther on the holiday of Purim, and to observe the prohibitions of the Torah – for instance, to fast on Yom Kippur and not to work on Shabbat or holidays. Also, she's obligated to study and to grow religiously.

Adulthood

I went to a Jewish wedding with my mom and dad. The bride and groom got married under a canopy. Why?

The canopy, called a *"chupah"* in Hebrew, is a cloth held up by four poles. (Sometimes people hold the poles.) The *chupah* is symbolic of a house. The bride and groom are united in this little house because they're making a home and a life together. Usually the *chupah* is placed under the open sky. That's to show that the wedding takes place before heaven and the watchful eye of God. But there's

The Chupah

another reason why Jews have weddings outdoors. In the past, anti-Semites watched synagogues in order to disrupt the weddings.

WHEN DID THIS HAPPEN? AND WHERE?

It happened in ancient times in Israel during the Roman occupation, and much later in the seventeenth, eighteenth, and nineteenth centuries in Hungary, in the Ukraine, and possibly in other places.

BUT HOW COULD THE JEWS HIDE WEDDINGS OUTDOORS? ANYBODY COULD COME ALONG.

The anti-Semites couldn't watch the whole outdoors. They didn't know what was going on in the woods.

CAN A JEW MARRY SOMEONE WHO'S NOT JEWISH?

Judaism does not permit marriage between Jews and

non-Jews, not because a non-Jew is less of a person, but because Judaism is a religion of the home and family. In fact, the home is considered the sanctuary of Judaism, more than the synagogue. Because Judaism is something you do all the time, it's almost impossible to have a full Jewish life in a home where one partner practices another religion. Therefore, Jews are urged to marry only within their faith.

Do you have to have a rabbi to get married?

You don't have to, but it's better to have a rabbi, someone knowledgeable in Jewish law who makes sure the marriage is performed without mistakes.

Death

What's a Jewish funeral like?

There's no open coffin, for one thing. The person who died isn't put on view. That's because Judaism is devoted to life, and teaches us to remember people as they were at their best, not after their life has been taken from them. The mourners, meaning the family of the person who died, tear a garment, like a sweater, a shirt, or a jacket. That's to show that their hearts are torn. Near the end of the funeral, the friends of the person who died bury him. They actually put the dirt in the grave on top of the coffin. It's the last thing we do for someone we care about. Why allow strangers to do it? We want to do it. And at the very end of the funeral, the mourners recite a prayer called the *"kaddish."* The word kaddish means holy. It praises God at a time when we may feel angry at Him for having taken someone we love.

But if you're angry, why do you want to praise God?

It's natural to be angry with God on occasion, but when we do, we need to find a way back to Him. In this case, the kaddish prayer provides the opportunity.

ARE JEWS CREMATED?

It's forbidden in Jewish law. Jews believe that the body is a shrine, a holy place, and should be left to take its natural course after God separates it from the soul. But there's another reason why we find cremation repulsive. Throughout history, anti-Semites have burned Jews. During the most recent example, the Holocaust, probably between four and five million Jews were burned in crematoria, or ovens. The Nazis, like other oppressors in history, wanted to make sure nothing was left to prove Jews once existed. So from a historical perspective, Jews find cremation abhorrent.

I'VE SEEN WHITE JEWISH CANDLES IN THE GROCERY STORE. WHAT ARE THEY FOR?

They're not Jewish candles, of course. They're just candles. On Friday evening, eighteen minutes before the sun sets, the woman of the house, or the man if he lives alone, lights two candles to welcome the Sabbath. Some light more candles, one for each member of the household.

WHAT DO THE CANDLES MEAN?

Candles are lit before all major Jewish holidays – Passover, Sukkot, Shavuot, Rosh Hashanah and Yom Kippur. The light of the candles represents the light of Torah, of knowledge. This is how we Jews make anything in our lives holier, by bringing more understanding, which in turn brings us closer to God and to our fellow Jews and to other people in the world. Light also brings joy because for us, knowledge is the most joyous human experience.

Chapter Six

JEWISH BELIEFS

Religion

Is Judaism a religion?

Judaism is a religion – the national religion of the Jewish people – but it's more than that. It's practices from the Torah, the Talmud, and from books known as the Codes, which are a systematic collection of Jewish laws. We believe these laws were given by God.

What happens to Jews who change their religion? Do you still call them Jews?

According to Jewish law, Jews who convert to other religions are considered Jews for two generations, meaning they and their children. But they can't be included in a congregation or be part of a religious service. In the early

1960's the Supreme Court of the state of Israel went further. It ruled that Jews who change their religion can no longer be considered part of the Jewish people.

Where does the word "Judaism" come from?

The word Judaism comes from "Judah." In the Bible we read that Jacob told his son Judah: "The scepter shall never part from Judah." Hundreds of years later a member of the tribe of Judah by the name of David became the first Judaean king of Israel. (Saul, the previous king, was a member of the tribe of Benjamin.) About a hundred years later the kingdom was divided and the Judeans, loyal to the House of David, formed the kingdom of Judea, and ten of the other tribes formed the kingdom of Israel. The people of the kingdom of Israel did not practice the Biblical religion. Those in the kingdom of Judea continued, though not consistently, to follow the religion of King David, which became known as Judaism, or the religion of Judea.

Can you be a Jew and not believe in God?

You are a Jew if you are born of a Jewish parent, specifically a Jewish mother, or if you are a convert, meaning a person who has accepted the religion. So, you are a Jew even if you don't believe in God, but you are not a religious Jew.

Why do you have to have a Jewish mother, and not a Jewish father?

When a child is born, we're sure who the mother is, but sometimes we don't know who the father is. Also, by the laws of nature a woman gives birth to a child, nurses it, and though not in all cases, raises the child. She exerts the greatest influence biologically and emotionally. Therefore, the Talmud determined thousands of years ago that the identity of the child would be based on the mother, not the father.

BUT WHAT IF SCIENCE COULD PROVE THAT THE FATHER IS JEWISH? WOULD THAT CHANGE JEWISH LAW?

No. We believe that Jewish law is for all time. We don't change it to accommodate new technologies.

WHAT'S THE PURPOSE IN BEING JEWISH?

It's the repair of the world, what in Hebrew we call "*tikkun olam*." That means bringing God into the world. But we don't force God on people. We don't pass out little pamphlets on street corners. We bring God into the world by practicing our religion, which means observing the mitzvot, or commandments.

WHY DO YOU THINK JEWS SHOULD BE RELIGIOUS?

If we don't feel accountable before an all-knowing God, no law in the world can stop us from inflicting hurt on other people.

WHAT LANGUAGE IS THE TORAH WRITTEN IN?

Hebrew.

DO YOU BELIEVE THAT GOD SPOKE TO MOSES IN HEBREW?

Yes.

DOES THAT MEAN HEBREW PRAYERS GET TO GOD FASTER THAN PRAYERS IN OTHER LANGUAGES?

I don't believe prayers reach God faster or better if they are in Hebrew. We Jews pray in Hebrew because we want to be connected with other Jews throughout the world and with previous generations of Jews. Also, we pray in Hebrew because it's the original language and we want to say the right words. But God understands every language. He spoke to Moses in Hebrew because that was the language Moses understood. And once God spoke the words, Hebrew became the holy tongue. However, there were some rabbis several thousand years ago who taught that while the Torah was given in Hebrew, it was also given in every known language in the world at that time.

Why don't we have miracles today?

The Talmud says that in ancient times our ancestors were prepared to die for their beliefs. We no longer have that level of passion, so we don't see miracles.

Do Jews believe in angels?

There is a discussion of angels in both the Bible and the Talmud. So, yes, Jewish tradition accepts that angels exist.

What do they do?

There are ministering angels who serve God and perform different tasks for Him. For instance, there is an angel named Raphael who heals for God. And there is an angel who defends humans before the heavenly court. And according to one legendary source, there is an angel for every mitzvah and for every sin.

Do Jews believe in guardian angels?

Yes. This comes from the verse in Genesis, "May the angel who redeems me from all evil bless the young ones." Many Jews recite this verse on Friday nights when they return home from the synagogue and bless their children. But there's little discussion among Jewish scholars about angels. It's not a significant part of our beliefs.

Do you think that people can see angels?

No.

Why not? Abraham in the Bible saw them, didn't he?

Yes, and so did the prophet Ezekiel in his vision of the chariot going up into heaven. But we can no longer see angels today for the same reason we can no longer see miracles. We are not endowed with *"ruach hakodesh,"* the holy spirit (unlike our ancestors, who were willing to die for their beliefs).

Do Jews believe in heaven?

Yes. We believe that after death is judgment. Some people go to *Gan Eden*, what others call paradise or heaven. This is the eternal reward where souls live forever. And some people go to *gehinnom*, what others call purgatory or hell. This is where people are punished for the wrongs they committed in life. We also believe that God is compassionate and only punishes those who committed unforgivable crimes, such as spreading hate or committing murder.

What does "Gan Eden" mean?

Garden of Eden.

Do you have to be Jewish to go there?

No. Jewish tradition does not teach that Jews have the exclusive right to salvation. People who are righteous, and who deal justly and lovingly with others, have as much right to heaven as a good Jew.

What will people do in heaven?

We believe that the righteous will sit in the presence of God, study the Torah, and enjoy a delight that words cannot describe or humans understand.

Do Jews believe that people go to heaven right after they die, or later?

According to Jewish tradition, judgment occurs at the hour of death or close to it. There are different views on this, and we are taught not to speculate.

Judaism is a life-oriented religion. The rewards we seek are in this world.

Do Jews believe in a resurrection?

Yes, but unlike Christians, we believe that the Messiah has yet to come. We wait for him to lead us to Israel – the promised land – and bring peace into the world. Then God will bring the dead back to life. That's the resurrection.

Who gets resurrected?

Those who have lived a righteous and decent life.

Can you go to heaven and still be resurrected?

Yes. Life after death is immediate, while the resurrection is something which will happen on earth in a post-Messianic age. Resurrection is the hardest thing a Jew is called upon to believe, but it is mandatory and one of the thirteen beliefs a Jew says after the weekday morning prayers: "I believe with perfect faith that at the time that God may want it, the dead will come back to life."

Who wrote the thirteen beliefs?

They were written by one of the greatest rabbis who ever lived, Maimonides, or Rabbi Moshe the son of Maiman. He lived about 850 years ago.

What do Jews think the world will be like after the Messiah comes?

There will no longer be any wars. As Isaiah taught, "Nation shall not lift up sword unto nation, nor will they learn war anymore." People will live in peace, and love will prevail in the world. Everyone will recognize that there is only one God, the God of Abraham, Isaac and Jacob.

What will the Messiah be like?

The Messiah will be a person. According to one Talmudic opinion, he will be a very poor person who rides a donkey. Also, he will be a descendant of King David, from the tribe of Judah. He will be the king of the Jews, chosen by God, but with nothing divine or godlike about him.

So if somebody dies and goes to heaven, he waits around for the Messiah to come, then he gets resurrected and comes back to earth?

Yes, and the resurrection is one reason why Jews oppose cremation, because the very body in which we are buried will come back to life. It will come back as it was at its prime, meaning when we were healthiest, handsomest, or prettiest.

It sounds like earth is more important in Jewish belief than heaven.

"Neither the dead can praise God nor any who descend into silence. But we will bless God from this time and forever." That's a verse from Psalms. It means we should make this world the happiest, best place we can – if possible, forever. It means we should put an end to death.

How?

By using all the means of science and medicine.

Science

But how do Jews reconcile science with religious ideas, like resurrection and heaven?

We don't have to reconcile them. Science applies to what we can, and eventually will, understand. Faith applies to what we will never understand. And the beginning of scientific exploration is faith. The scientist has to have faith that she can open up the hidden mysteries of life and find their meaning and truth even though none appear to her today.

Do Jews believe in evolution?

There is a view in the Talmud that man originally had two sides, one side with the face and front of the human body, the other side with a tail. So it is possible to accept the Torah and at the same time to accept Darwin's theory of evolution. But science constantly changes to accommodate new discoveries, while the Torah doesn't change.

Do Jews believe in the Big Bang?

We believe that God created the world about 5,760 years ago, but we also believe that God created many worlds. The Talmud tells us that He built them and destroyed them. This might fit in with what modern science teaches about the age of the earth because according to this Talmudic view, life can go back thousands, hundreds of thousands, if not millions of years. Perhaps God used what modern science thinks of as the Big Bang to create these worlds, so here again, there's really no conflict between science and the Bible.

Do Jews still believe in an eye for an eye?

Jews never believed in an eye for an eye. The Torah is the written law, and Jews read the Torah based on the Talmud, the oral law. The Talmud explains that an "eye for an eye" or a "tooth for a tooth" means compensation. In other words, if you put out my eye, you pay for my medical treatments and other damages.

The Bible

IS THE JEWISH BIBLE THE SAME AS THE CHRISTIAN OLD TESTAMENT?

Not entirely because the Christian Old Testament is read in translation and the Jewish Bible is read in its original language, Hebrew. The King James version and newer Christian translations are based on a translation from Greek to English. Since the Greek is not the same as the Hebrew, many of the words in the Jewish Bible and Christian Old Testament have different meanings, and thus different messages. Also, we depend on the Talmud, or the oral law, to give us the actual meaning of each word in the Bible.

ARE YOU SAYING THAT AN ENGLISH TRANSLATION OF THE JEWISH BIBLE WOULD BE DIFFERENT FROM AN ENGLISH TRANSLATION OF THE CHRISTIAN OLD TESTAMENT?

Yes.

WHY DON'T JEWS HAVE THE NEW TESTAMENT IN THEIR BIBLE?

That would be abandoning our religion and accepting a new one.

WHAT DO YOU MEAN?

In Judaism all the laws of the Torah, or what Christians call the Old Testament, are obligatory. We must practice them. Regarding the food laws, for example, we must refrain from eating pork, shellfish, and meat cooked with milk. In the New Testament, Paul said no one had to observe these laws anymore and only had to believe in the new version of God. In essence, he asked Jews to abandon Judaism.

ARE THERE JEWISH MISSIONARIES?

Judaism doesn't send out missionaries. According to

the Torah, people who aren't Jewish don't have to become Jewish or keep the mitzvot in order to go to heaven. They only have to keep the seven laws of Noah and his three sons, the survivors of the biblical flood, and thus the ancestors of all people. These "Noachide Laws" include not killing, stealing, worshiping idols, eating the flesh of living animals, or committing immorality, such as incest.

Food

Is chicken soup Jewish?

Well, people think it is, but chickens aren't born Jewish. And plenty of non-Jews eat chicken soup.

Why don't Jews eat pork?

The Torah forbids us to eat pork because the pig doesn't chew its cud, one characteristic of a kosher animal. Also, the Torah specifically says, "And the swine you shall not eat." Maimonides said that the natural habitat of the pig is a filthy one. In the days of the Bible, people lived with the animals they ate and adopted their habits. So maybe God didn't want us to adopt the uncouth habits of pigs. But the basic reason Jews don't eat pork is because God said not to.

Do Jews eat only kosher foods?

Orthodox Judaism teaches that Jews should only eat kosher foods, both in their homes and in public. Conservative Judaism teaches the importance of keeping kosher, while Reform Judaism does not accept the laws of kosher food.

Can you tell if a food is kosher by looking at it?

You can, if it's a packaged food because it will have a symbol printed on it that tells you it's kosher. Raw foods, such as milk, eggs, fruits or vegetables, are kosher without a symbol.

Chapter Six

Where do you buy kosher food?

Ordinary supermarkets sell raw kosher foods, and kosher butchers and delicatessens sell meats and poultry. In some cities supermarkets have special sections for processed kosher foods, like frozen chicken parts, matzot, stuffed fish.

How is a Jewish deli different from a regular deli?

A Jewish deli, if it's really Jewish, is kosher. It maintains the food laws of Judaism. And the first thing you notice in a kosher deli is the separation of meat and dairy products because kosher laws forbid mixing the two.

What makes meat and dairy products kosher?

The meat products – steaks, tenderloins, chuck roasts, hamburger, ribs, lamb chops – come from cows and lambs, animals that chew their cud and have split hooves. These animals have been slaughtered in the most painless and quick way possible, as required by Jewish law.

The poultry products – duck, chicken, turkey – come from birds permitted by the Torah (twenty birds are specifically forbidden.) They too have been slaughtered in the most painless and quick way possible, as required by Jewish law.

The fish products – trout, salmon, red snapper, perch – come from fish that have fins and scales.

The dairy products – cheese, ice cream, cakes, cookies, candies – are manufactured with all kosher ingredients and contain no meat derivatives, such as lard.

And finally, the old types of Jewish foods you see in a deli are really not Jewish but Eastern European, Polish, Russian, or Hungarian. Corned beef, for example, was a German food Jews adopted. Hot dogs or frankfurters probably came from Germany as well, maybe from Poland. Pastrami came from Romania.

Chapter Seven

The Jewish People

Do you have Jewish priests?

In one sense, yes. The first priest in the Bible was Aaron, the brother of Moses. All his children were priests, what in Hebrew we call *"kohanim."* They said certain blessings, acted as physicians, brought sacrifices and other offerings to the Tabernacle, and later to the Temple in Jerusalem. But they never functioned as religious leaders.

Isn't a rabbi a Jewish priest?

No. A rabbi is a teacher and leader of his community, one who gives advice to his congregants and delivers sermons. Unlike Christian clergy, rabbis don't necessarily lead the prayers during worship services because every Jew can pray to God without a representative.

Can women be rabbis?

In Conservative, Reform, and Reconstructionist Judaism, women can be rabbis, but not in Orthodox Judaism. According to the Torah, men should imitate Moses, the first rabbi in history, who was a leader and judge. Orthodox women have different roles.

You mean like being a wife and mother? Isn't that sexist?

Orthodox women aren't just wives and mothers. They are doctors, lawyers, teachers, writers, musicians, business leaders, or anything else they want to be. But in religious life, men serve as rabbis.

So an Orthodox woman who is a teacher can't teach about Judaism?

Although Orthodox women can't be rabbis, they can be as learned as, if not more learned than, any rabbi. The most respected Jewish Bible scholar in the contemporary world was a woman by the name of Nechama Leibowitz, a professor at Hebrew University in Israel. Sadly, she died in 1997, but there are more women scholars like her, and they are growing in number here and in Israel.

Why do some Jewish men wear little caps?

Originally, the only Jewish person who wore this hat was the High Priest in the Temple in Jerusalem, who needed to be reminded that God was above him. Later, it became a practice for all Jewish men and boys to wear some sort of hat as a reminder that regardless of who they were, God was higher.

The hat is called a *yarmulke* in Yiddish and *kippa* in

Wearing A Kippa

Hebrew. Some people think the word is derived from Russian or Polish, but it comes from two Hebrew words, *"yerah me-Elokim,"* fear of God.

How does a yarmulke remind you that God is higher?

Whenever I look at myself or touch my head, I feel something there. That lets me know God is above me. But there's another reason why I, or any Jewish man, wear a yarmulke, and that's to say publicly, "I am Jewish."

Do Jewish boys wear their yarmulkes when they go swimming?

No. Jewish boys and men are not required to wear their yarmulkes when they sleep or when they bathe, and swimming is like bathing.

Is it true that some Jewish women shave their heads and wear wigs?

Some married Jewish women cover their hair out of modesty, since hair can be considered an enticement. If they wear a wig, rather than a scarf or hat, and the wig is difficult to put on, those women will shave their heads.

Why are there so many famous Jewish violinists?

Someone once said that the sound of the violin is like crying. Perhaps Jews, having suffered for two thousand years, play the violin because it's a way for them to turn their crying into music. But not only famous violinists are Jewish. A large number of pianists, conductors, and composers are Jewish as well. And Jews have excelled in other forms of art, such as painting and writing. I think it's because Jews are a passionate people.

Why?

So much in Judaism is based on the commandments to love, for example, "And thou shalt love the Lord thy God with all thy heart," and "You shall love your fellow as yourself." Much of the ritual of Judaism, like praying three times a day, requires a love of God and Torah. And there is a tradition of compassion among Jews, to give money to the poor and to pray for the sick, so it's no surprise that Jews gravitate towards the arts where they can express deep emotions. And bear in mind that Jews are commanded to love a God who has no physical body. That makes us emotional, as well as intellectual, in our approach to life.

Why are so many doctors Jewish?

In the days of the Bible, the *kohanim*, or priests, served as doctors. Healing the body was considered more important than healing the soul because a healthy body served God better. The implication of the verse from Psalms, "Not the dead can praise God, but only the living," is that we should live as long as possible, and help others live as long as possible. Therefore, medicine is one of the holiest professions in Judaism, and some of the most renowned rabbis in history were doctors, including Maimonides.

The symbol of the snake on a pole has become synonymous with healing and medicine. Many people find the origin of this symbol in the Torah in the book of Exodus 4:1-5 and 7:8-12 when God told Moses to throw his staff to the ground, and it turned into a serpent.

WHAT DOES IT MEAN THAT JEWS ARE THE CHOSEN PEOPLE?

We believe God chose the Jews to be the teachers of His law. And the way we are to teach is by example, not by words. We hope that by observing the mitzvot, we will lead the rest of the world to believe in God, and to act justly and mercifully. So "chosen" means chosen to have a particular responsibility, not chosen to be above or better than anyone else.

DO YOU THINK GOD LOVES THE JEWS MORE THAN HE LOVES OTHER PEOPLE?

The prophets say yes, that God chose us because He loved us. As Isaiah put it, even when we fail to follow God's teachings, He loves us and hopes we will return to Him, like an errant child to his parent. But according to the Talmud, all the righteous people of the world are beloved by God.

A Final Word from Rabbi Grossman to Kids

The two largest religions in the world, Christianity and Islam, have their roots in Judaism. And most of what we call civilization, belief in law and family, has its roots in Judaism. Not all good ideas come from Jews, of course, but it's important to know the origin of what you believe.

And because so much comes from Jews, knowing about them will enrich your life. Not knowing about them will make you afraid of them. Part of the hatred directed towards Jews over the years has been the result of ignorance. People didn't know what the Jews did, or why they did it. And people, kids included, need to know that the Jews' mission is to inspire others, regardless of their religion or age, to godly behavior.

Rabbi Grossman was always available to answer questions.

When we Jews say hello and goodbye, we use an old Hebrew word, "*shalom*." But shalom doesn't mean hello, and it doesn't mean good-bye. It means "peace." That's my final word to kids, and that's the Jewish message to the world.

Rabbi Rafael Grossman

For almost thirty years Rabbi Rafael Grossman was the Senior Rabbi of Baron Hirsch Congregation, at the time, the largest Orthodox congregation in America.

A past president of the Beth Din of America, he was also a past president of the Rabbinical Council of America, chairman of the Rabbinical Council International, a national vice-president of the Religious Zionists of America, co-chairman of the Rabbinic Cabinet of Israel Bonds, and a member of the Executive Board of the Union of Orthodox Jewish Congregations of America.

(R-L) Rabbi Rafael Grossman addressing the press with Rabbi Yisrael Meir Lau, the Ashkenazi Chief Rabbi of Israel

Rabbi Grossman was the author of *Binah, the Modern Quest for Torah Understanding* and wrote a regular column that appeared for many years in *The Jewish Press* newspaper. Two of his stories became the basis of books for young readers, the middle grade novel *Greenhorn* and the graphic novel *A Visit to Moscow*.

Rabbi Grossman died in Jerusalem in 2018.

Notes

(Use separate paper for your notes if this is not your book.)

www.ingramcontent.com/pod-product-compliance
Lightning Source LLC
LaVergne TN
LVHW051514090426
835512LV00010B/2528